WOMEN IN HIP-HOP

QUEENS OF THE MIC

CROWN SHEPHERD
CICELY LEWIS, EXECUTIVE EDITOR

LERNER PUBLICATIONS ◆ MINNEAPOLIS

LETTER FROM CICELY LEWIS

Dear Reader,

Hip-hop has been a part of my life from an early age. I remember using my brush as a microphone and rapping along with Salt-N-Pepa. Hip-hop influenced my fashion, way of speaking, and lifestyle. As a teacher, I shared Tupac's writings to teach poetry elements and Queen Latifah's "U.N.I.T.Y." to help my students better understand the works of poet Maya Angelou.

CICELY LEWIS

As a librarian, I want to expose my students to literature that empowers them to take action and that amplifies voices of underrepresented groups. That is what hip-hop does. Hip-hop is more than beats and rhymes; it's a cultural force. For Black people, it's been a spotlight on social justice, and a canvas for our frustrations, joys, and creativity.

As you read the series, think about the power of hip-hop and how it all began. You've probably heard of Cardi B and Nicki Minaj, but who paved the way for them? Reflect on how this musical genre that began in the Black Community is now present around the world.

—Cicely Lewis, Executive Editor

TABLE OF CONTENTS

CELEBRATING WOMEN EMCEES 4

CHAPTER 1
WOMEN WHO PAVED THE WAY 6

CHAPTER 2
GIRL POWER 12

CHAPTER 3
RECORD BREAKERS 17

CHAPTER 4
THE NEW GENERATION 22

GLOSSARY 28

SOURCE NOTES 29

READING LIST 30

INDEX 31

CELEBRATING WOMEN EMCEES

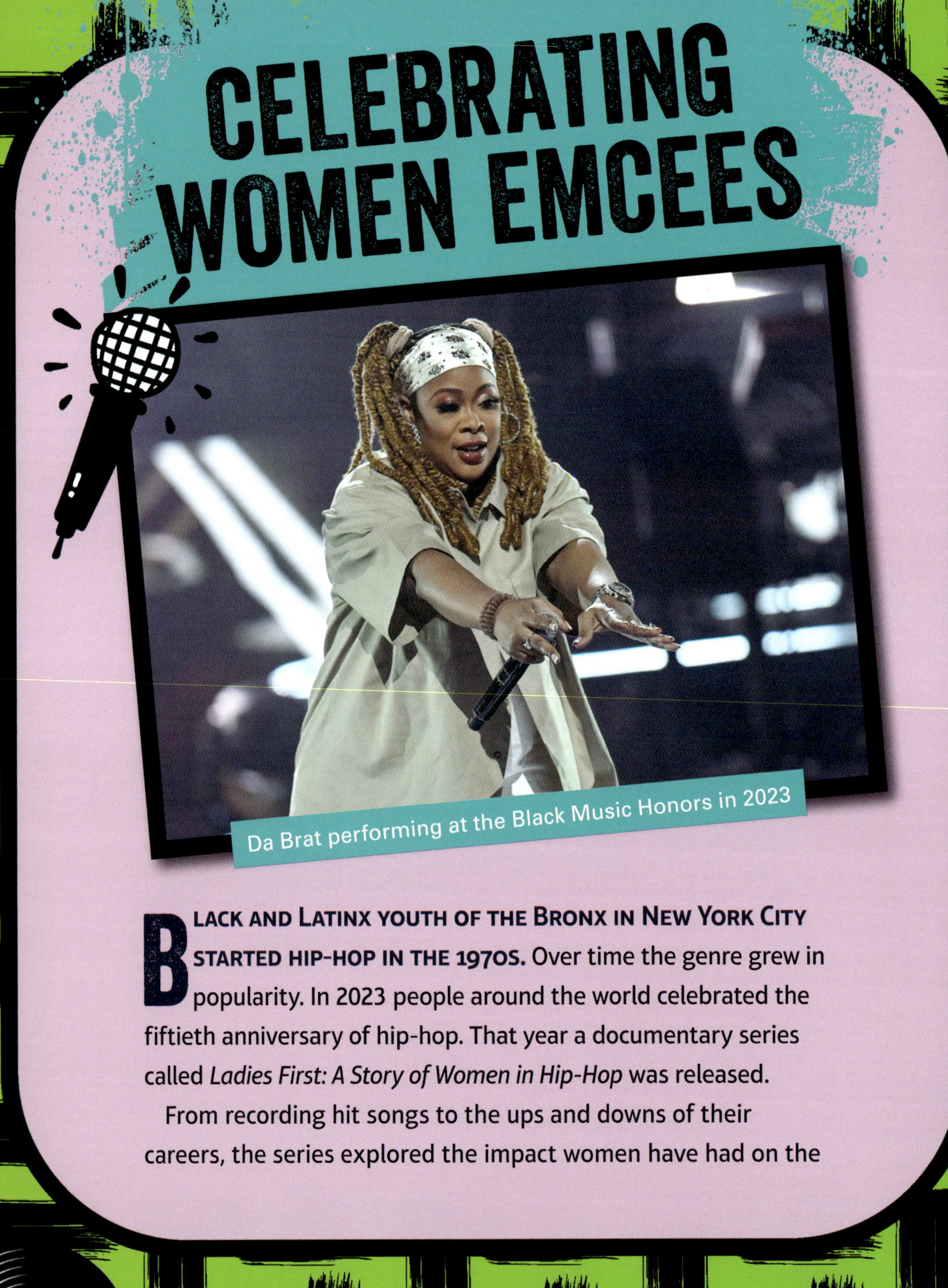

Da Brat performing at the Black Music Honors in 2023

BLACK AND LATINX YOUTH OF THE BRONX IN NEW YORK CITY STARTED HIP-HOP IN THE 1970S. Over time the genre grew in popularity. In 2023 people around the world celebrated the fiftieth anniversary of hip-hop. That year a documentary series called *Ladies First: A Story of Women in Hip-Hop* was released.

From recording hit songs to the ups and downs of their careers, the series explored the impact women have had on the

Cardi B attends the 2023 Met Gala.

world of hip-hop. It also highlighted the accomplishments of female emcees, or rappers, such as Da Brat, MC Lyte, Cardi B, and Latto. The women featured in the documentary showed love and admiration for one another.

Whether they are battling for their spot at the top, rapping about confidence, or making history, women have been vital to shaping hip-hop. The women in this book are among some of the greatest emcees in history.

CHAPTER 1

WOMEN WHO PAVED THE WAY

Queen Latifah performing at the 2019 MTV Video Music Awards

WOMEN HAVE BEEN PART OF HIP-HOP SINCE ITS BEGINNING. They have had great success in building the genre and setting the stage for more rappers.

A Funky 4 + 1 flyer

MOTHER OF THE MIC

Many people consider Sharon Green, or MC Sha-Rock, to be the Mother of the Mic and the first female rapper in hip-hop history. She inspired other artists such as the hip-hop group Run-D.M.C.

As a member of the hip-hop group Funky 4 + 1, she became the first female rapper to get a record deal. The group signed with Enjoy Records in 1979. Two years later, the group performed live on the sketch comedy show *Saturday Night Live*. It made MC Sha-Rock the first woman in hip-hop to perform on national TV.

"I mean, just being out there in the street and just listening to some of this, the sounds and the music and the percussion—it just gave you a feeling like you could just take on the world. It just empowered you as a woman."

—MC Sha-Rock

MC Lyte at an event in 2023

GOLD SINGLE

Lana Michele Moorer, or MC Lyte, released her first album, *Lyte as a Rock*, in 1988. It was the first solo album by a female rapper to be released from a major record label. In 1993 the popular song "Ruffneck" from her fourth album earned MC Lyte her first Grammy nomination for Best Rap Solo Performance. The song sold five hundred thousand copies, making it the first gold single for a female rapper.

In 2006 MC Lyte became the first solo female artist to join VH1's Hip Hop Honors. The event celebrates rappers for their role in hip-hop culture.

THE FIRST DIS TRACK

In 1984 Lolita Shanté Gooden, or Roxanne Shanté, released "Roxanne's Revenge" and sparked the Roxanne Wars. The Roxanne Wars led to thirty-five different artists making songs. Many people consider "Roxanne's Revenge" to be the first dis song—a song meant to insult a person or group—in hip-hop.

Roxanne Shanté putting on a show in 1988

Queen Latifah visits her star on the Hollywood Walk of Fame.

MAJOR AWARD WINNER

Dana Owens is an award-winning singer and actor known as Queen Latifah. She rapped about issues affecting Black women. Her popular song "U.N.I.T.Y" won the Best Rap Solo Performance Grammy Award in 1995. Queen Latifah was the first solo female artist to win in a rap category.

In 1991 Queen Latifah started acting. She later earned an Oscar nomination for her performance in the 2002 movie *Chicago*. In 2005 Queen Latifah hosted the Grammy Awards, becoming the first rapper to host the event. And, in 2006, Queen Latifah became the first rapper to receive a star on the Hollywood Walk of Fame.

Da Brat performing at KMEL Summer Jam in 1994

PLATINUM STAR

In 1992 Shawntae Harris, also known as Da Brat, won a rap contest called *Yo! MTV Raps*. The prize from this contest was to meet hip-hop duo Kris Kross. They introduced her to producer Jermaine Dupri. Da Brat ended up signing with Dupri's record label, So So Def Recordings.

In 1994 she released her first album, *Funkdafied*. The single of the same name spent twenty weeks on *Billboard* Hot 100, which charts the week's most popular songs. The album went platinum, making Da Brat the first solo female rapper to sell one million copies.

REFLECT

Many female emcees achieved firsts in hip-hop. Why is it important to learn about their achievements?

CHAPTER 2

GIRL POWER

Left to right: Rappers Lil' Kim, MC Lyte, and Remy Ma put on a performance at the 2006 VH1 Hop Hop Honors.

USING THEIR POWERFUL VOICES AND STATEMENT-MAKING LYRICS, WOMEN IN HIP-HOP HAVE BEEN SELLING OUT STADIUMS AND MAKING REAL CHANGE FOR WOMEN WITH THEIR ONE-OF-A-KIND MUSIC.

A PLATINUM ALBUM

Inga DeCarlo Fung Marchand is also known as Foxy Brown. As a teenager, she won a talent show in Park Slope, New York. It began her career in hip-hop. In 1995 she was featured on LL Cool J's song "I Shot Ya." A year later, she signed with the record label Def Jam Recordings. Her debut album, *Ill Na Na,* achieved platinum status.

Rapper Foxy Brown

REFLECT

Why do you think music is a powerful tool for uplifting others? What are some ways you think music can help spread awareness of certain topics?

EMPOWERMENT

Yolanda Whitaker, or Yo-Yo, is best known for her raps about women's empowerment. Yo-Yo was featured on Ice Cube's 1990 song "It's A Man's World." That song was her break into hip-hop. Her first album, *Make Way for the Motherlode,* was released in 1991.

Yo-Yo performing in 1991

GREAT ENTERTAINER

Melissa Viviane Jefferson, also known as Lizzo, is a talented rapper and flutist who often plays the flute in her songs. Lizzo worked with different music groups before going solo. In 2013 Lizzo released her debut solo album, *Lizzobangers*.

Lizzo gives her acceptance speech at the Grammy Awards in 2020.

Her 2017 song "Truth Hurts" became popular and spent seven weeks at number one on the *Billboard* Hot 100 chart. In 2019 *Time* named Lizzo Entertainer of the Year. As of 2025, she had thirteen Grammy nominations and had won four Grammy Awards.

"I was so excited about all the women in 2019. Being a Black woman is popping, but like right now in mainstream culture, like we're finally getting a little bit more respect and getting our due."

—Lizzo, 2019

CHAPTER 3

RECORD BREAKERS

Missy Elliott performs in 1998.

WOMEN HAVE ALWAYS MADE THEIR PRESENCE KNOWN IN HIP-HOP, SETTING OR BREAKING RECORDS AND MAKING HISTORY.

Missy Elliott joins the Songwriters Hall of Fame in 2019.

PLATINUM STAR

Four-time Grammy Award-winner Melissa Elliott, also known as Missy Elliott, wrote and produced songs before she started rapping. She even started her own record label called Goldmind. In 1997 she released her first album, *Supa Dupa Fly*. That same year, *Rolling Stone* named her Rap Artist of the Year.

In 2019 Elliott became the first female rapper to join the Songwriters Hall of Fame. She has released six studio albums. In 2022 she set a new record for most platinum albums by a female rapper with all of her albums going platinum.

ONE-HIT WONDER

Singer and actor Lauryn Hill began her hip-hop career with the Fugees, a hip-hop trio. In 1993 the group signed a record deal with Ruffhouse Records. The group released two albums before splitting up in 1997.

Lauryn Hill celebrates winning a Grammy Award in 1999.

In 1998 Hill released her first and only solo album, *The Miseducation of Lauryn Hill*. Over four hundred thousand copies were sold in its first week. The album would sell over twenty million copies worldwide and go multiplatinum. Hill won five Grammy Awards, including Album of the Year. She became the first woman to win five awards at a single Grammys ceremony.

HISTORIC GRAMMY NIGHT

In 2010 Beyoncé broke Lauryn Hill's record by having the most Grammy wins in one night. Beyoncé won six Grammys, including Song of the Year. As of 2025, she had been nominated for ninety-nine Grammy Awards and had won thirty-five Grammys. Her music blends genres such as pop, hip-hop, R&B, and country.

Beyoncé performing at the Grammy Awards in 2010

CHART CLIMBER

Nicki Minaj in 2011

Onika Maraj, commonly known as Nicki Minaj, wrote her first rap song when she was twelve years old. In 2007 Minaj started gaining attention after releasing her first mixtape, *Playtime Is Over.* In 2008 she won the Female Artist of the Year award at the Underground Music Awards. The Underground Music Awards is an award show honoring unsigned and independent artists.

In 2009 she signed her first record deal with Young Money Entertainment. She released her first album, *Pink Friday,* a year later. As of 2025, Minaj had 149 songs on the *Billboard* Hot 100 chart.

REFLECT

How do you think female emcees have shaped hip-hop as a whole? What can we learn from their achievements?

CHAPTER 4

THE NEW GENERATION

Cardi B wins a Grammy Award in 2019.

HIP-HOP IS ALWAYS CHANGING AND GROWING. Newer artists are trying to make a name for themselves and leave their mark in the music world.

Megan Thee Stallion with her Grammy Awards in 2021

TRADEMARKED

In 2016 Megan Pete, also known as Megan Thee Stallion, started releasing mixtapes. Her 2019 song "Hot Girl Summer" featured Nicki Minaj and Ty Dolla $ign. The hit song went double platinum. The term "Hot Girl Summer" became so popular that Megan Thee Stallion got it trademarked.

In 2020 Megan Thee Stallion's song "Savage" went viral on social media with a dance challenge. She won three Grammy Awards in 2021. Two of the awards, Best Rap Performance and Best Rap Song, were for "Savage."

Cardi B performing at an event in 2023

THE REALITY STAR

Belcalis Marlenis Almánzar, or Cardi B, started her career as a social media influencer. In 2015 she starred on *Love & Hip Hop: New York*. The reality TV show followed women who wanted to be rappers.

Cardi B signed her first record deal with Atlantic Records in 2017. Soon after, she released "Bodak Yellow." The song reached number one on the *Billboard* Hot 100 and Hot R&B/Hip-Hop Songs charts. In 2018 she released her first studio album, *Invasion of Privacy*. The next year, Cardi B won the Best Rap Album Grammy Award. She was the first female solo rapper to win the award.

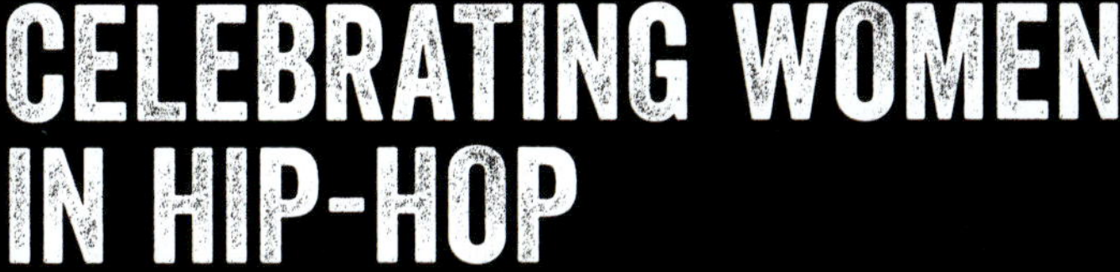

CELEBRATING WOMEN IN HIP-HOP

In 2022 MC Lyte presented at the first I Am Woman: A Celebration of Women in Hip Hop. The event celebrates female emcees and their contributions to hip-hop music. The event featured performances by several female hip-hop artists, including Da Brat.

MC Lyte accepts an award in 2022.

Latto performing at the 2023 Coachella Valley Music and Arts Festival

HUGE SINGLES

When she was sixteen years old, Alyssa Stephens, or Latto, won a rapping reality TV show called *The Rap Game*. She turned down her first record deal from So So Def Recordings to be an independent artist.

In 2019 she released her first EP. An EP is a musical recording with more tracks than a single but fewer tracks than an album. In 2020 she signed with RCA Records. Later that year, she released her first album, *Queen of Da Souf*. One of the songs on the album went gold. Another song went platinum.

REFLECT

Why do you think it's important for new artists to make their mark in the hip-hop world?

In 2023 MC Sha-Rock performs at an event celebrating the fiftieth anniversary of hip-hop.

A BRIGHT FUTURE

Women have made their mark in hip-hop for decades. And new artists bring fresh ideas and sounds that shape the future of the music we love. Newer and older artists inspire other artists and fans, showing that anyone with a voice and a vision can make an impact on hip-hop.

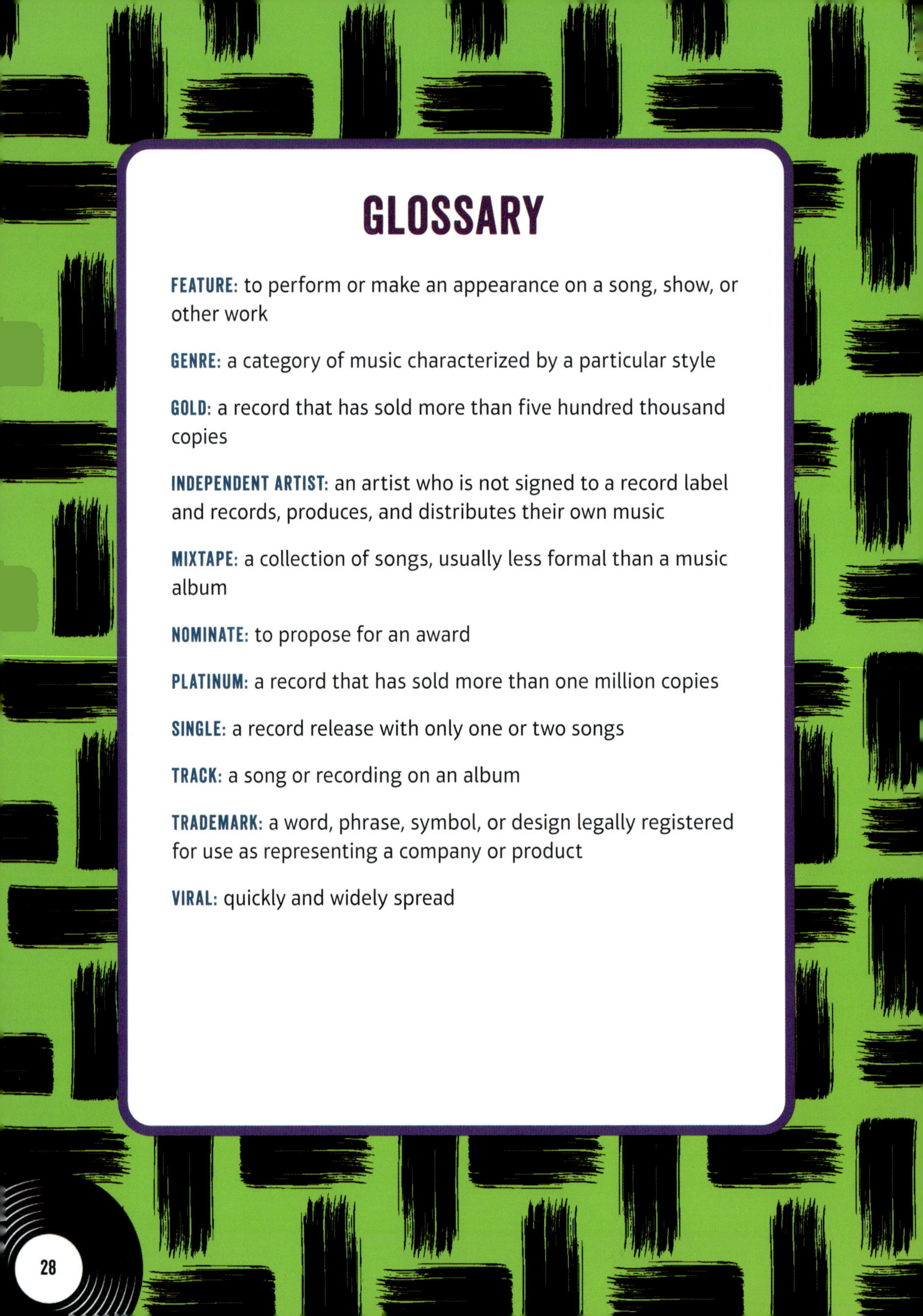

GLOSSARY

FEATURE: to perform or make an appearance on a song, show, or other work

GENRE: a category of music characterized by a particular style

GOLD: a record that has sold more than five hundred thousand copies

INDEPENDENT ARTIST: an artist who is not signed to a record label and records, produces, and distributes their own music

MIXTAPE: a collection of songs, usually less formal than a music album

NOMINATE: to propose for an award

PLATINUM: a record that has sold more than one million copies

SINGLE: a record release with only one or two songs

TRACK: a song or recording on an album

TRADEMARK: a word, phrase, symbol, or design legally registered for use as representing a company or product

VIRAL: quickly and widely spread

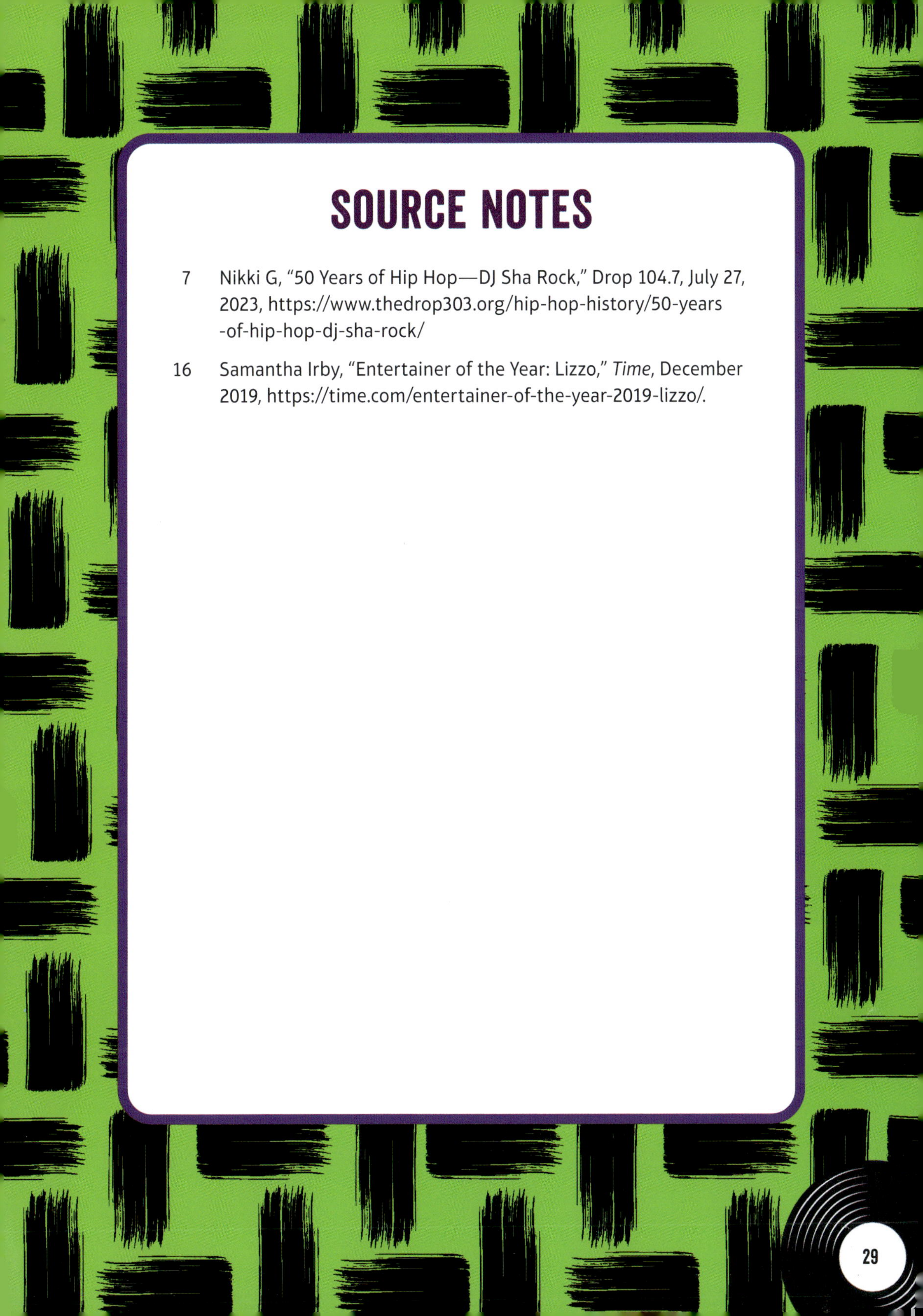

SOURCE NOTES

7 Nikki G, "50 Years of Hip Hop—DJ Sha Rock," Drop 104.7, July 27, 2023, https://www.thedrop303.org/hip-hop-history/50-years-of-hip-hop-dj-sha-rock/

16 Samantha Irby, "Entertainer of the Year: Lizzo," *Time*, December 2019, https://time.com/entertainer-of-the-year-2019-lizzo/.

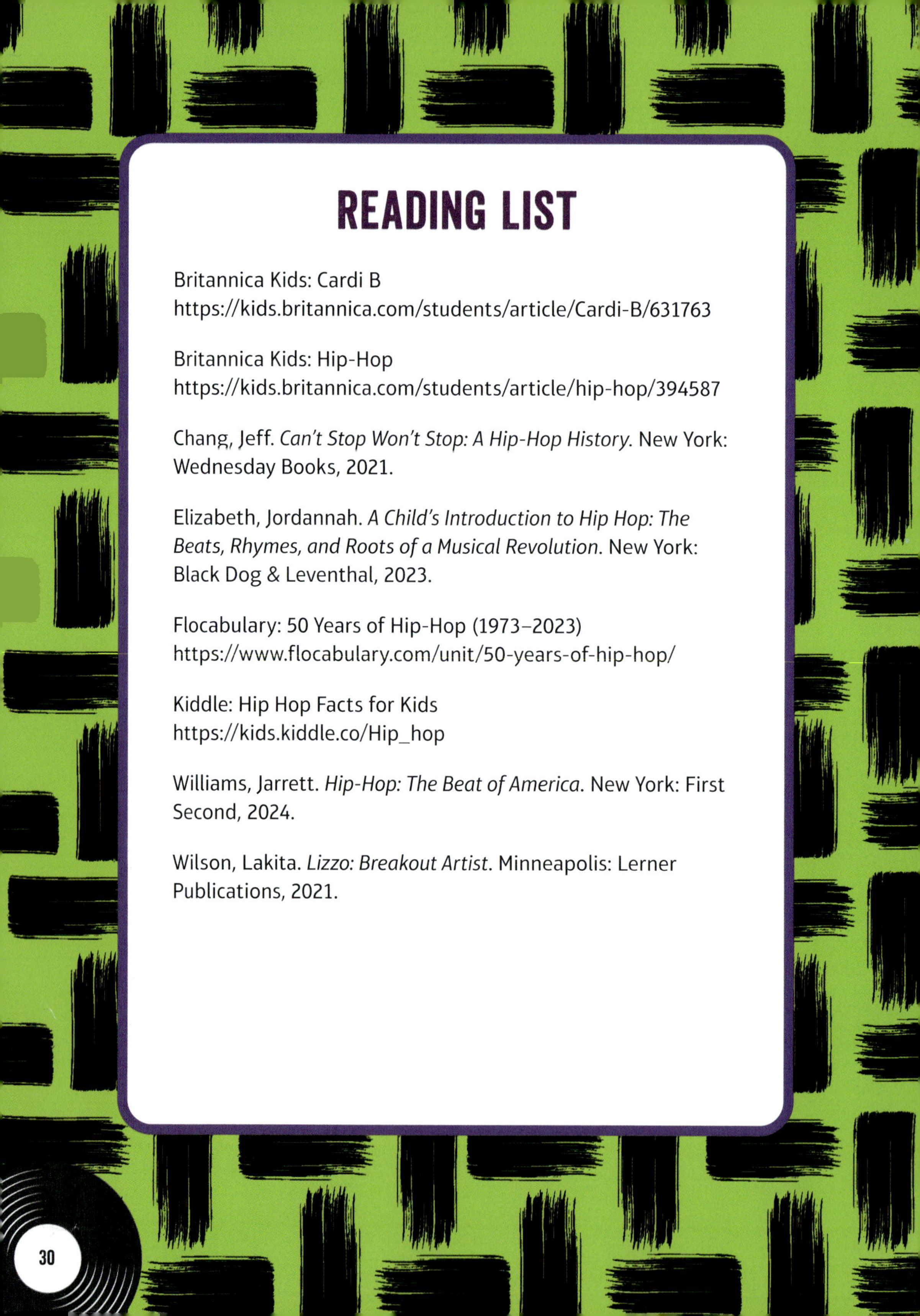

READING LIST

Britannica Kids: Cardi B
https://kids.britannica.com/students/article/Cardi-B/631763

Britannica Kids: Hip-Hop
https://kids.britannica.com/students/article/hip-hop/394587

Chang, Jeff. *Can't Stop Won't Stop: A Hip-Hop History*. New York: Wednesday Books, 2021.

Elizabeth, Jordannah. *A Child's Introduction to Hip Hop: The Beats, Rhymes, and Roots of a Musical Revolution*. New York: Black Dog & Leventhal, 2023.

Flocabulary: 50 Years of Hip-Hop (1973–2023)
https://www.flocabulary.com/unit/50-years-of-hip-hop/

Kiddle: Hip Hop Facts for Kids
https://kids.kiddle.co/Hip_hop

Williams, Jarrett. *Hip-Hop: The Beat of America*. New York: First Second, 2024.

Wilson, Lakita. *Lizzo: Breakout Artist*. Minneapolis: Lerner Publications, 2021.

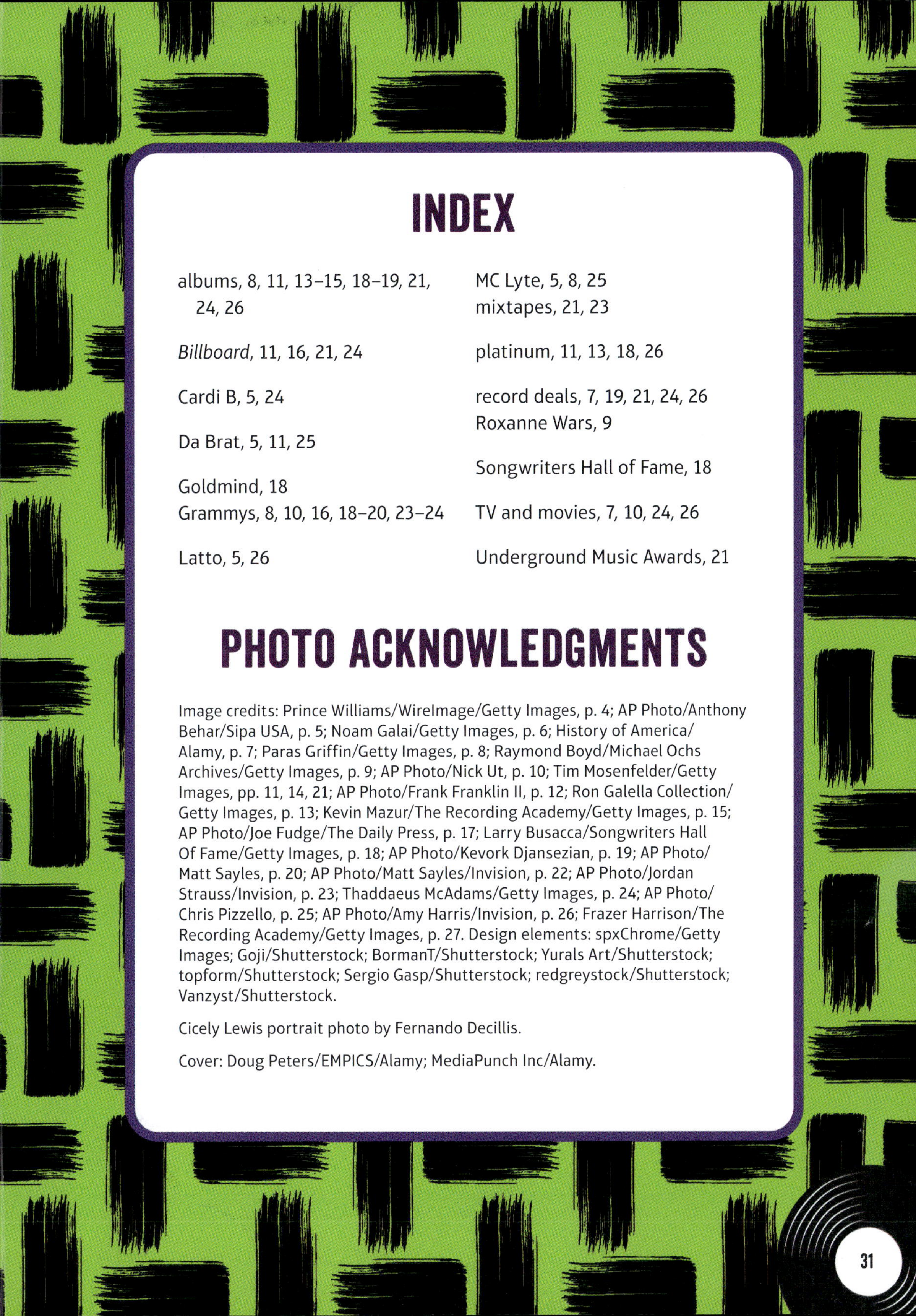

INDEX

albums, 8, 11, 13–15, 18–19, 21, 24, 26

Billboard, 11, 16, 21, 24

Cardi B, 5, 24

Da Brat, 5, 11, 25

Goldmind, 18
Grammys, 8, 10, 16, 18–20, 23–24

Latto, 5, 26

MC Lyte, 5, 8, 25
mixtapes, 21, 23

platinum, 11, 13, 18, 26

record deals, 7, 19, 21, 24, 26
Roxanne Wars, 9

Songwriters Hall of Fame, 18

TV and movies, 7, 10, 24, 26

Underground Music Awards, 21

PHOTO ACKNOWLEDGMENTS

Image credits: Prince Williams/WireImage/Getty Images, p. 4; AP Photo/Anthony Behar/Sipa USA, p. 5; Noam Galai/Getty Images, p. 6; History of America/Alamy, p. 7; Paras Griffin/Getty Images, p. 8; Raymond Boyd/Michael Ochs Archives/Getty Images, p. 9; AP Photo/Nick Ut, p. 10; Tim Mosenfelder/Getty Images, pp. 11, 14, 21; AP Photo/Frank Franklin II, p. 12; Ron Galella Collection/Getty Images, p. 13; Kevin Mazur/The Recording Academy/Getty Images, p. 15; AP Photo/Joe Fudge/The Daily Press, p. 17; Larry Busacca/Songwriters Hall Of Fame/Getty Images, p. 18; AP Photo/Kevork Djansezian, p. 19; AP Photo/Matt Sayles, p. 20; AP Photo/Matt Sayles/Invision, p. 22; AP Photo/Jordan Strauss/Invision, p. 23; Thaddaeus McAdams/Getty Images, p. 24; AP Photo/Chris Pizzello, p. 25; AP Photo/Amy Harris/Invision, p. 26; Frazer Harrison/The Recording Academy/Getty Images, p. 27. Design elements: spxChrome/Getty Images; Goji/Shutterstock; BormanT/Shutterstock; Yurals Art/Shutterstock; topform/Shutterstock; Sergio Gasp/Shutterstock; redgreystock/Shutterstock; Vanzyst/Shutterstock.

Cicely Lewis portrait photo by Fernando Decillis.

Cover: Doug Peters/EMPICS/Alamy; MediaPunch Inc/Alamy.

TO ALL THE POWERFUL WOMEN FROM THE PAST, THE PRESENT, AND THE FUTURE. REMEMBER WHAT YOU'RE CAPABLE OF.

Lerner Publications Company
An imprint of Lerner Publishing Group, Inc.
241 First Avenue North
Minneapolis, MN 55401 USA

For reading levels and more information, look up this title at www.lernerbooks.com.

Main body text set in Aptifer Sans LT Pro.
Typeface provided by Linotype AG.

Library of Congress Cataloging-in-Publication Data

Names: Shepherd, Crown, author.
Title: Women in hip-hop : Queens of the mic / Crown Shepherd.
Description: Minneapolis : Lerner Publications, 2026. | Series: Hip-hop culture | Includes bibliographical references and index. | Audience: Ages 9–14 | Audience: Grades 4–6 | Summary: "From record-breakers to activists, women rule the world of hip-hop. Discover the important women who have achieved firsts or set records in hip-hop. Then learn about the women who continue influencing the culture"— Provided by publisher.
Identifiers: LCCN 2024042763 (print) | LCCN 2024042764 (ebook) | ISBN 9798765684283 (paperback) | ISBN 9798765659878 (library binding) | ISBN 9798765678138 (epub)
Subjects: LCSH: Women rap musicians—Juvenile literature.
Classification: LCC ML82 .S54 2025 (print) | LCC ML82 (ebook) | DDC 782.421649092/52—dc23/eng/20240911

LC record available at https://lccn.loc.gov/2024042763
LC ebook record available at https://lccn.loc.gov/2024042764

Manufactured in the United States of America
1-1011688-53634-2/28/2025